# ESSENTIAL ELEMENTS for Band

**COMPREHENSIVE BAND METHOD**

TIM LAUTZENHEISER • JOHN HIGGINS • CHARLES MENGHINI
PAUL LAVENDER • TOM C. RHODES • DON BIERSCHENK

I0802865

These piano accompaniments can provide helpful guidance for teaching beginning instrumentalists. The format includes a cue line to provide the director or pianist with a visual guide of the student melody part.

The harmony and style of each piano example is compatible with online accompaniment tracks. These tracks are available online using the code included with student books and conductor books.

Each example also includes chord symbols for the director or pianist to adapt the written part as needed for specific teaching situations.

ISBN 979-835015516-7

HAL•LEONARD®
A Muse Group Company



Visit Hal Leonard Online at
**www.halleonard.com**

World headquarters, contact:
**Hal Leonard**
7777 West Bluemound Road
Milwaukee, WI 53213
Email: info@halleonard.com

In Europe, contact:
**Hal Leonard Europe Limited**
1 Red Place
London, W1K 6PL
Email: info@halleonardeurope.com

In Australia, contact:
**Hal Leonard Australia Pty. Ltd.**
4 Lentara Court
Cheltenham, Victoria, 3192 Australia
Email: info@halleonard.com.au

## 1. TECHNIQUE TRAX

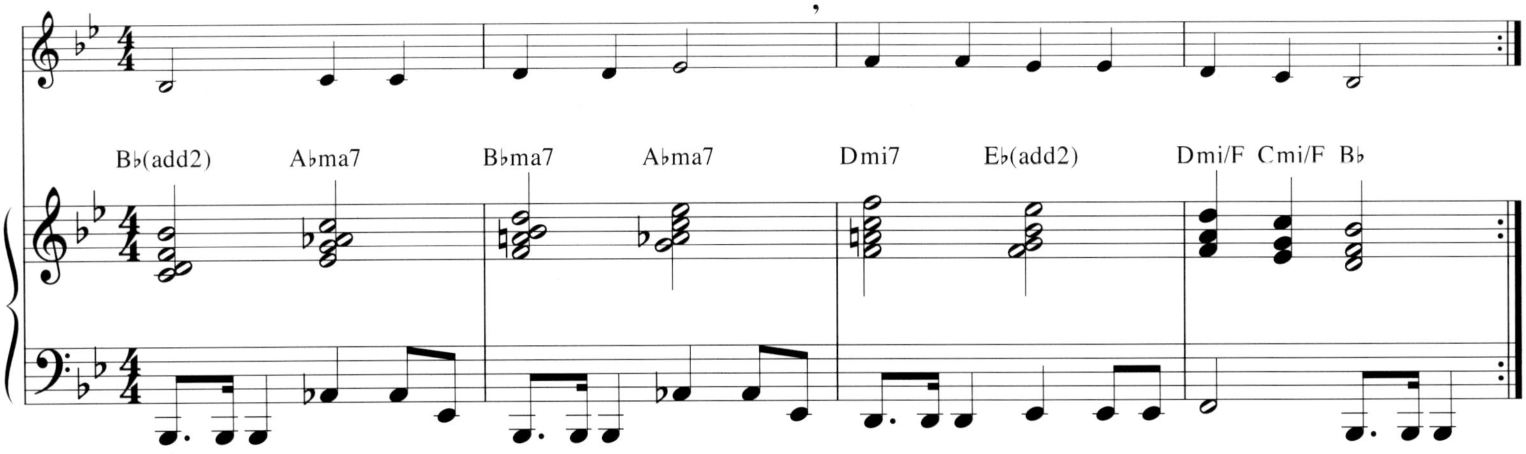


## 2. WELCOME SONG

FUNGA ALAFIA
African Folk Song

## 3. THAILAND LULLABY

Thai Folk Song

Moderato

## 4. SHEPHERD'S HEY

English Folk Song

Moderato

## 5. THE CRAWDAD SONG

American Folk Song

**Allegro**

## 6. AMERICA/GOD SAVE THE QUEEN

Based on a Traditional Anthem

## 7. WEARING OF THE GREEN

Irish Folk Song

## 8. ROSES FROM THE SOUTH

Johann Strauss, Jr.

## 9. CRUISIN' THROUGH THE PARK

## 10. TRUMPET VOLUNTARY — Duet

Jeremiah Clarke

## 11. CHROMA-ZONE

## 12. BILLY BOY

American Folk Song

## 13. TECHNIQUE TRAX

## 14. SALSA SIESTA – Duet

## 15. TREADING LIGHTLY

## 16. SMOOTH MOVE

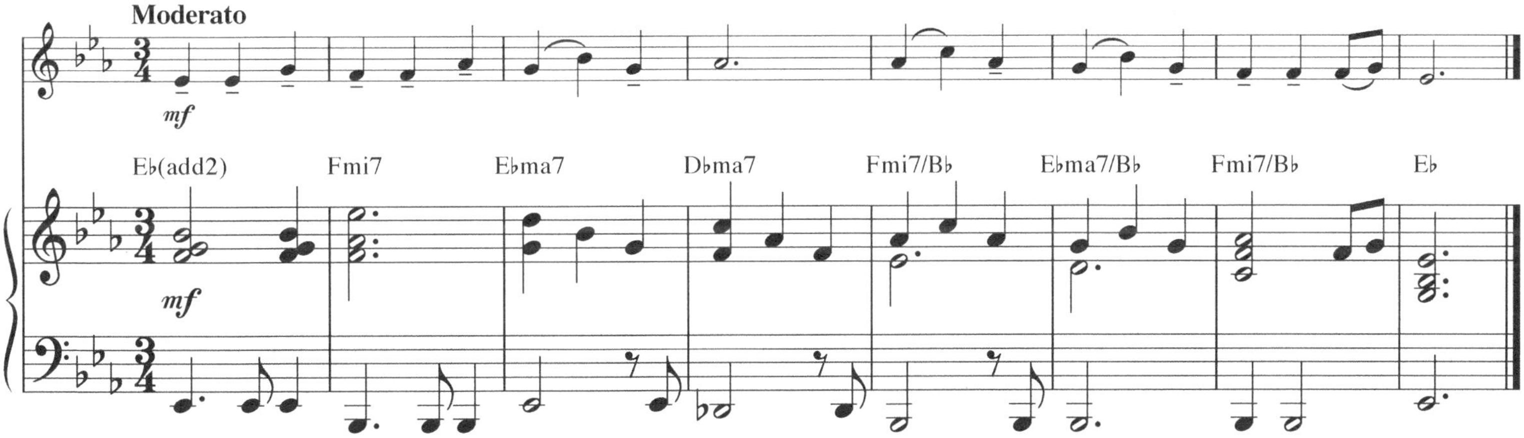


## 17. SHIFTING GEARS

## 18. TALLIS CANON (Round)

**Moderato**

Thomas Tallis

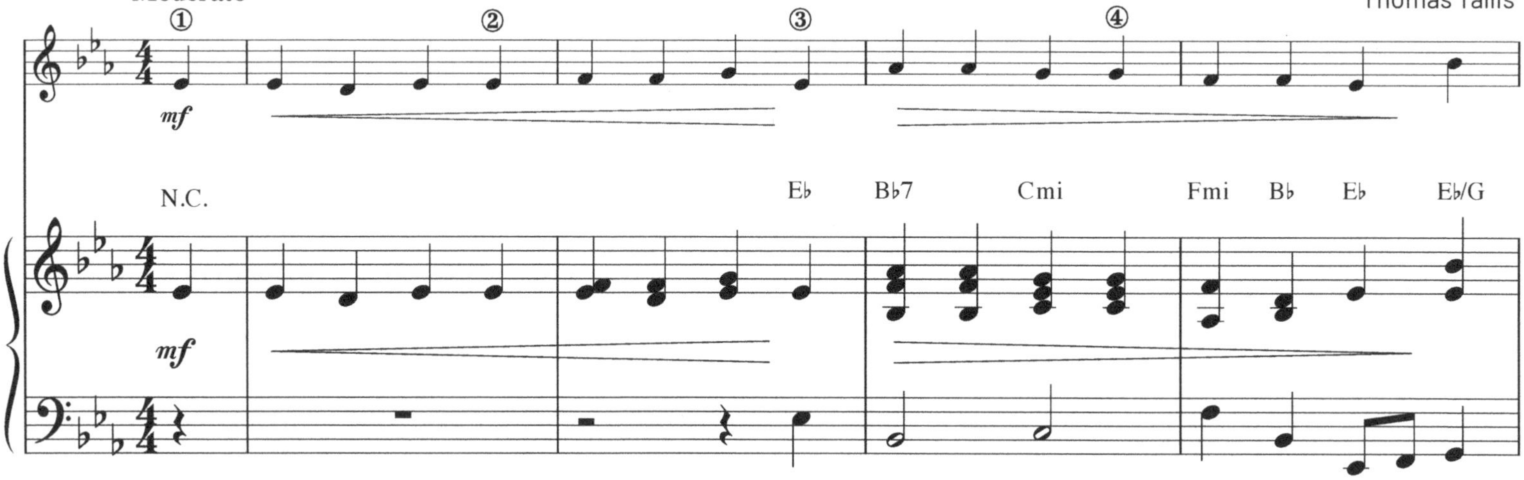

▼ *Student books end here. Extra mesures have been added to allow all 4 parts of the round to finish.*

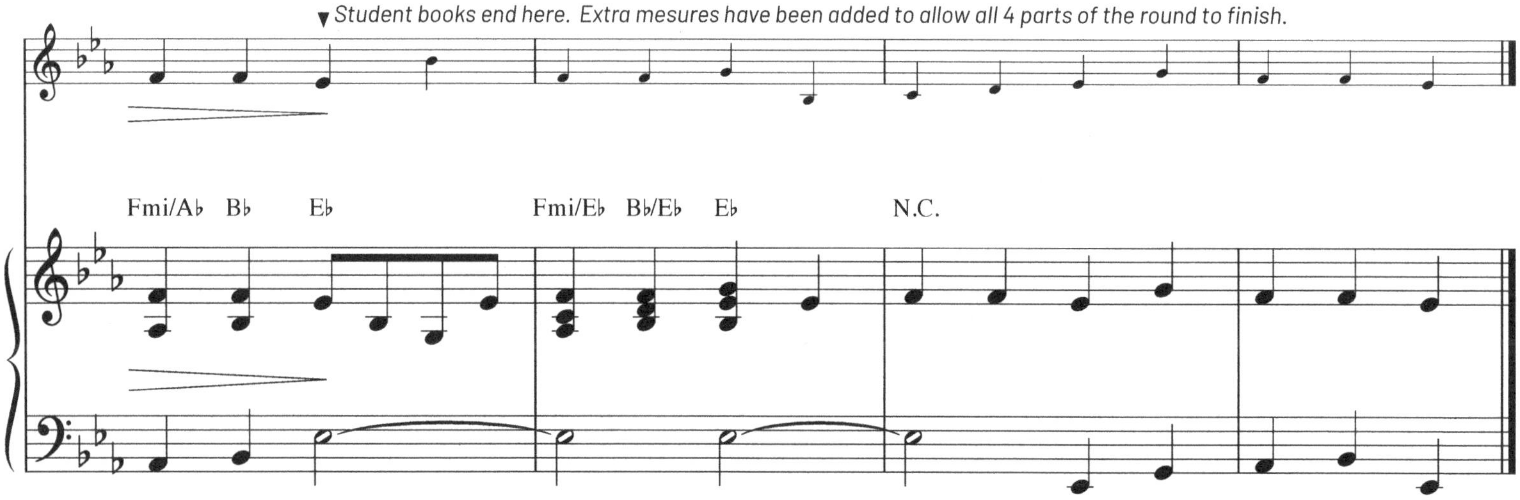

## 19. SIGHTREADING CHALLENGE

## 20. TONE BUILDER

## 21. FLEXIBILITY STUDY

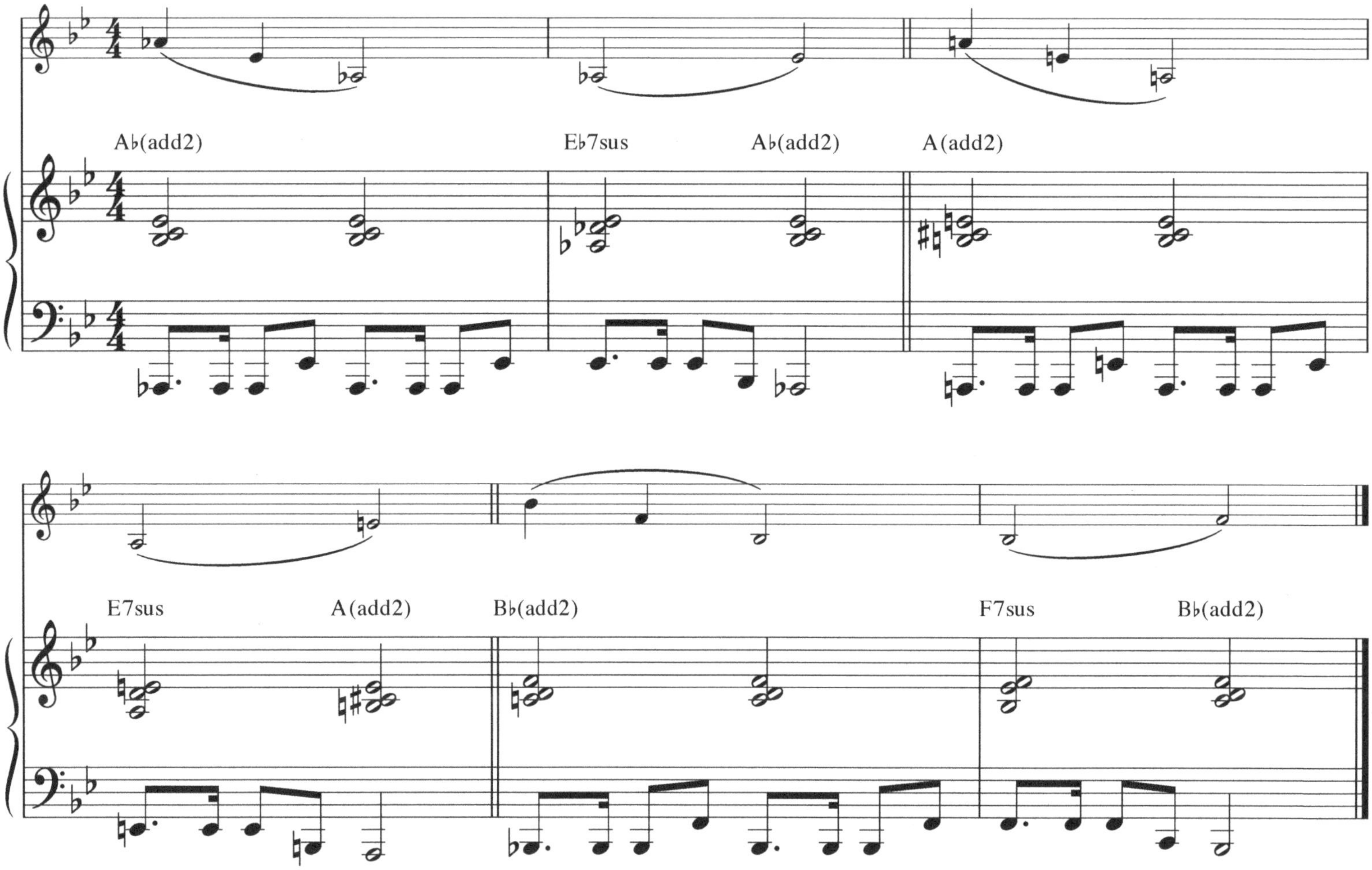


## 22. TECHNIQUE TRAX

## 23. CHORALE

Andante

Johann Sebastian Bach

## 24. GRANDFATHER'S CLOCK

Henry C. Work

## 25. GLOW WORM

Paul Lincke

## 26. ALMA MATER

A.C. Weekes, W.M. Smith, H.S. Thompson

## 27. LOCH LOMOND

## 28. MOLLY MALONE

Irish Folk Song

## 29. RISE AND FALL

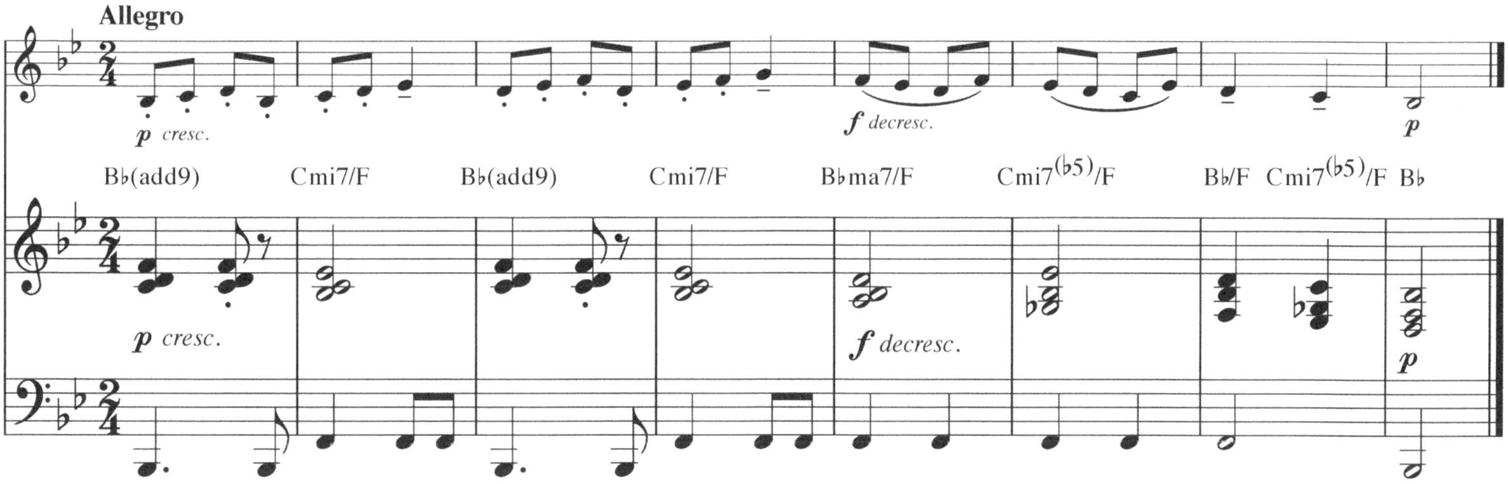


## 30. NO COMPARISON

## 31. SIGHTREADING CHALLENGE

## 32. RHYTHM RAP

## 33. A CUT ABOVE

## 34. TWO-FOUR YANKEE DOODLE

American Folk Song

## 35. CUT TIME YANKEE DOODLE

American Folk Song

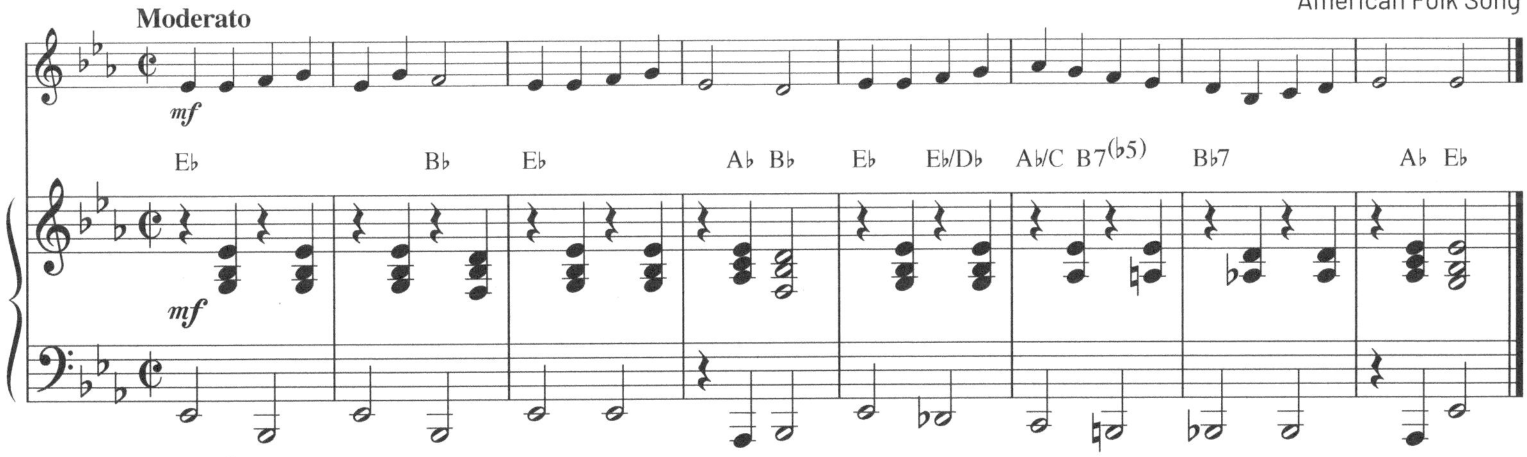


## 36. MARIANNE

Jamaican Folk Song

## 37. THE VICTORS

March Tempo

Louis Elbel

### 38. ESSENTIAL CREATIVITY

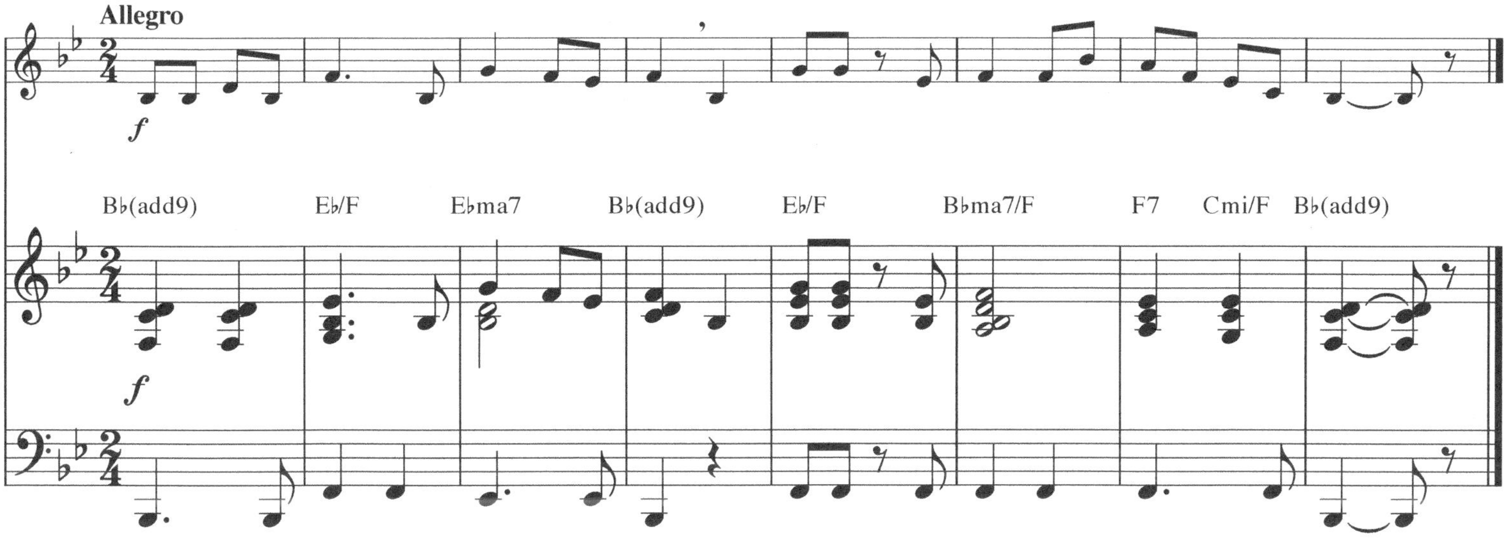


### 39. A - ROVING

### 40. RHYTHM RAP

## 41. IN SYNC

## 42. LA ROCA

Puerto Rican Folk Song

## 43. ESSENTIAL ELEMENTS QUIZ – YOU'RE A GRAND OLD FLAG

**March Style**

George M. Cohan

Student Book Page 10

## 44. KEY MOMENT

## 45. THE MINSTREL BOY

Irish Folk Song

## 46. CLOSE CALL

## 47. VICTORY MARCH

M. J. Shea

# 48. WINNING STREAK

M. J. Shea

March Tempo

## 49. SIGHTREADING CHALLENGE

## 50. RHYTHM RAP

*Student books have repeats, not 1st and 2nd endings.*

## 51. SIXTEENTH NOTE FANFARE

*Student books have repeats, not 1st and 2nd endings.*

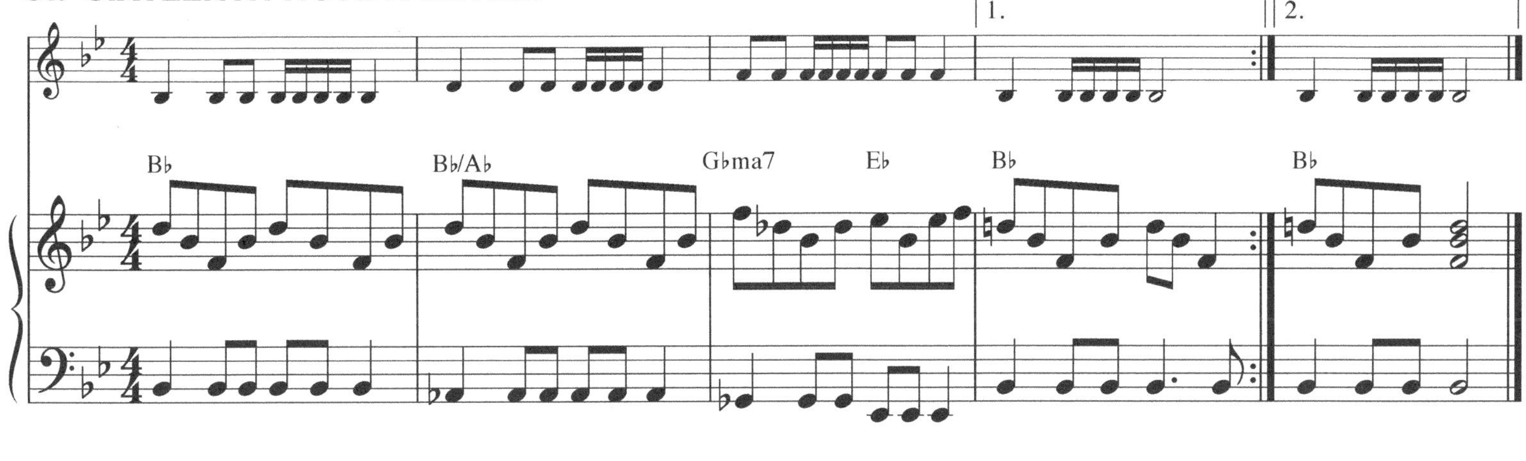

## 52. MOVING ALONG

*Student books have repeats, not 1st and 2nd endings.*

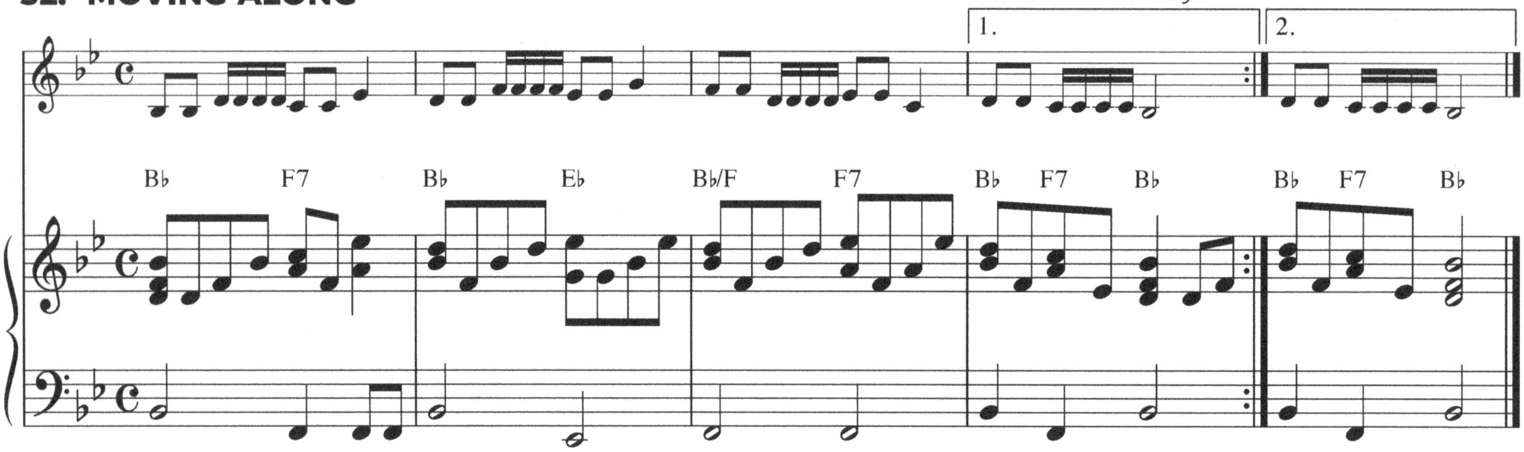


## 53. BACK AND FORTH – Duet

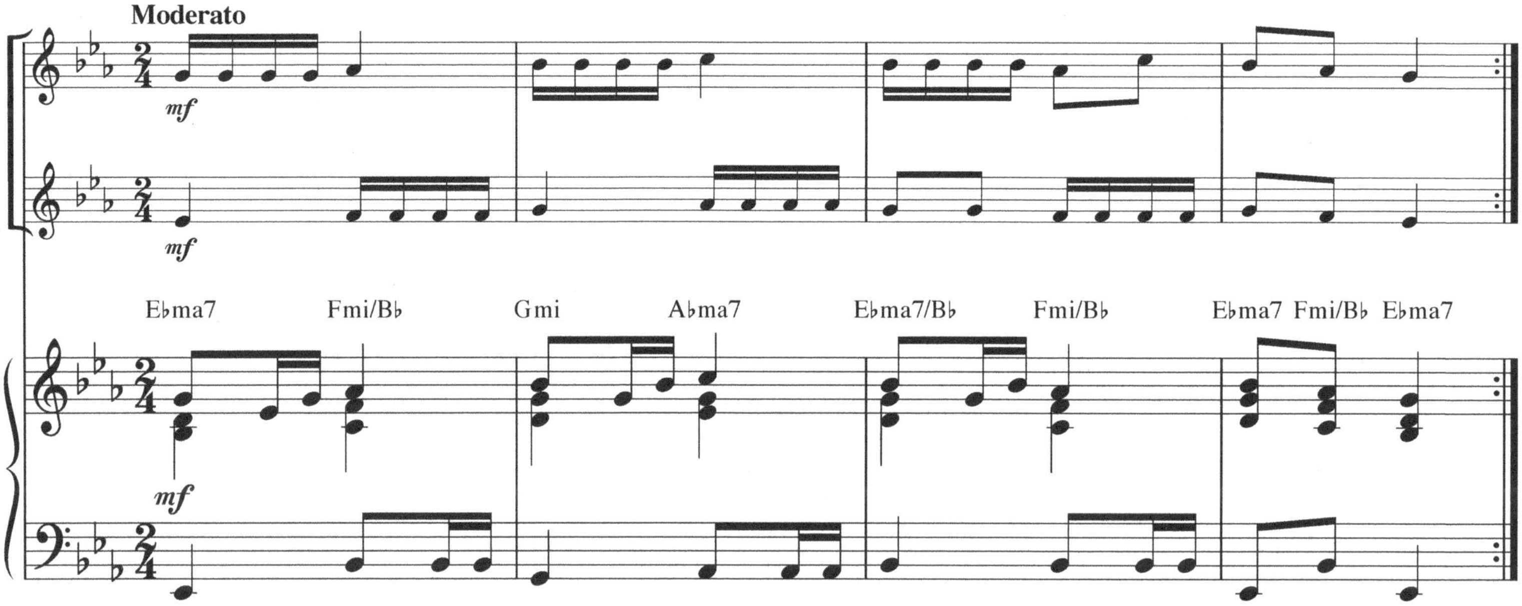


## 54. COMIN ' ROUND THE MOUNTAIN VARIATIONS

American Folk Song

## 55. ESSENTIAL ELEMENTS QUIZ

Moderato

## 56. WARM-UP CHORALE

J. S. Bach/Arr. by John Higgins

## 57. THE THUNDERER– Band Arrangement

John Philip Sousa
Arr. by John Higgins

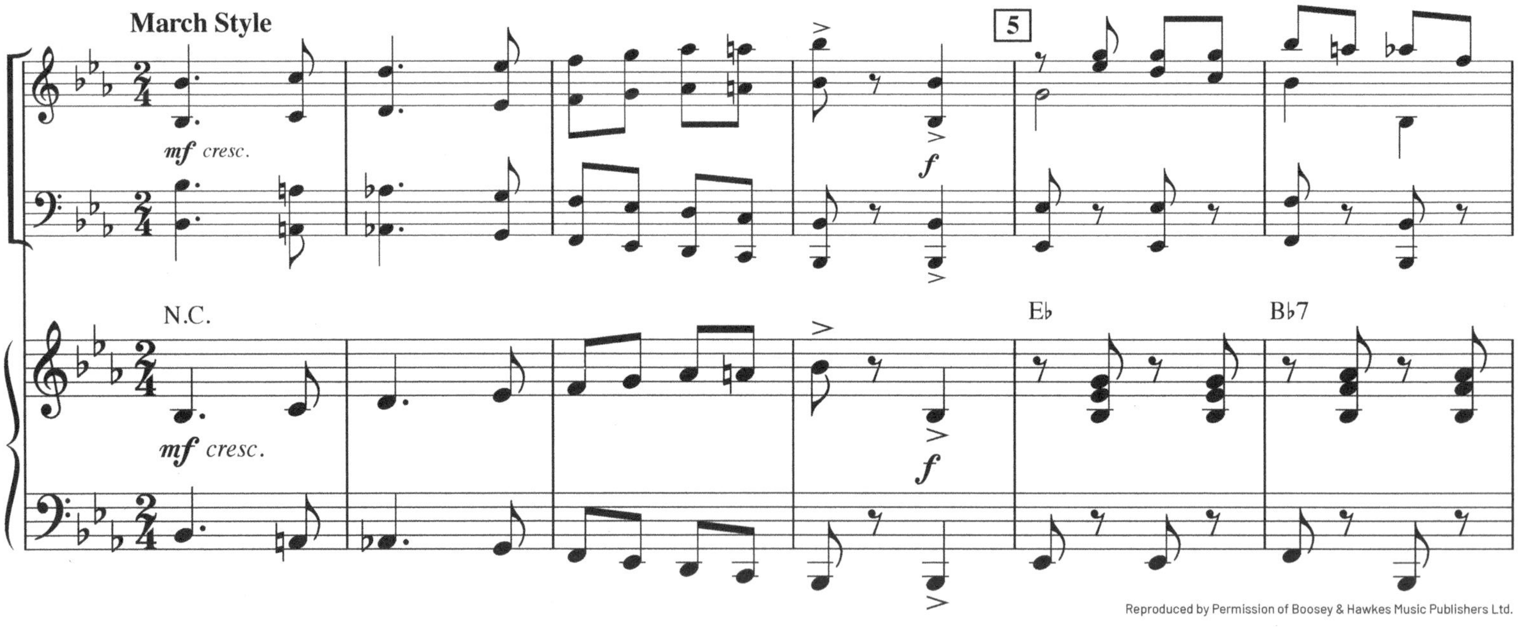

E♭
B♭7
13
E♭
B♭7
E♭
B♭7
Fine
D.C. al Fine
mf
N.C.
B♭
N.C.
B♭o
mf

## 58. HILL AND GULLY RIDER – Band Arrangement

Jamaican Folk Song
Arr. by John Higgins

## 59. SHENANDOAH – Band Arrangement

American Folk Song
Arr. by John Higgins

## 60. LAS MAÑANITAS – Band Arrangement

Mexican Folk Song
Arr. by John Higgins

19
F/C Bb/C C7
F
C7
F
C7
F
p
cresc.
Bb
F Dmi
F/C Bb/C C7
F
F
f
(b)
1.
2.

Student Book Page 13

## 61. RONDEAU – Band Arrangement

Jean-Joseph Mouret
Arr. by John Higgins

D.S. al Fine
N.C.

## 62. ROCK.COM – Encore Band Arrangement

Moderato

John Higgins

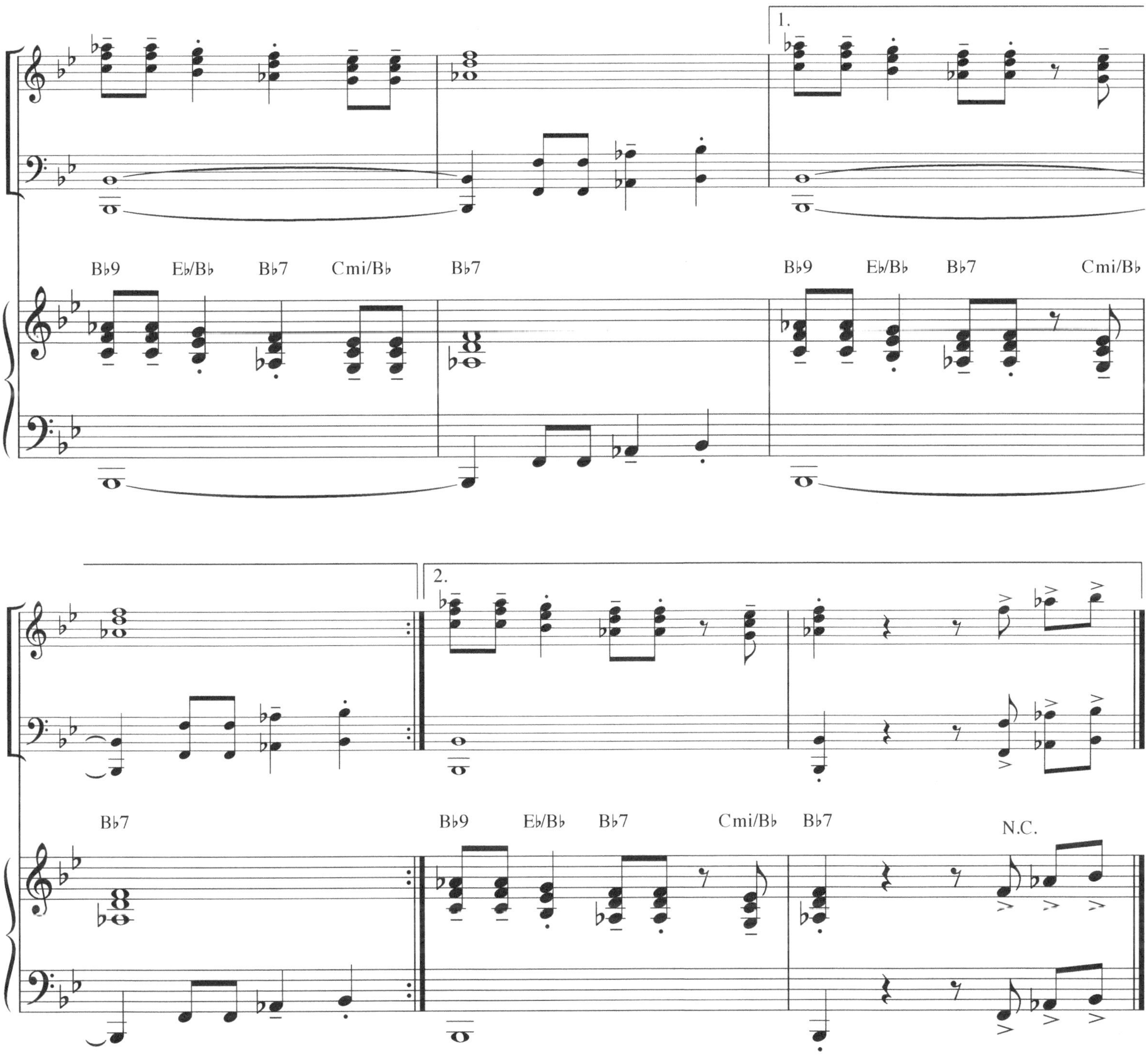
1.
B♭9
E♭/B♭
B♭7
Cmi/B♭
B♭7
B♭9
E♭/B♭
B♭7
Cmi/B♭
2.
B♭7
B♭9
E♭/B♭
B♭7
Cmi/B♭
B♭7
N.C.

## 63. RHYTHM RAP

## 64. SIXTEENTH VARIATIONS

## 65. SEA CHANTEY

Student books have repeats, not 1st and 2nd endings.

## 66. AMERICAN FANFARE

## 67. SCALE STUDY

## 68. BILL BAILEY

Hughie Cannon

## 69. RHYTHM RAP

## 70. RHYTHM ETUDE

## 71. BATTLE STATIONS

## 72. ENGLISH DANCE

## 73. BIG ROCK CANDY MOUNTAIN

American Folk Song

## 74. ESSENTIAL ELEMENTS QUIZ

## 75. SIMPLE SONG – Duet

Adagio

## 76. LINE DANCE

Allegretto

*Student books have repeats, not 1st and 2nd endings.*

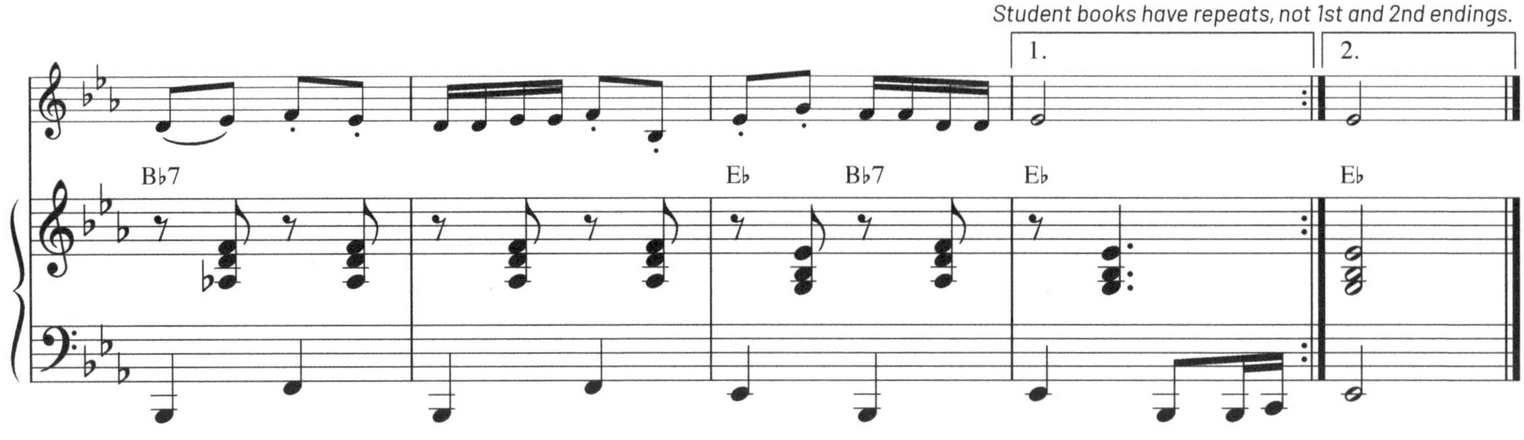

## 77. TECHNIQUE TRAX

Moderato

## 78. THE GALWAY PIPER

Irish Reel

Moderato

*Student books repeat the 1st 8 measures.*

## 79. MANHATTAN BEACH MARCH

John Philip Sousa

## 80. SIGHTREADING CHALLENGE

## 81. RHYTHM RAP

## 82. MARCHING ALONG

## 83. FANFARE FOR BAND – Trio

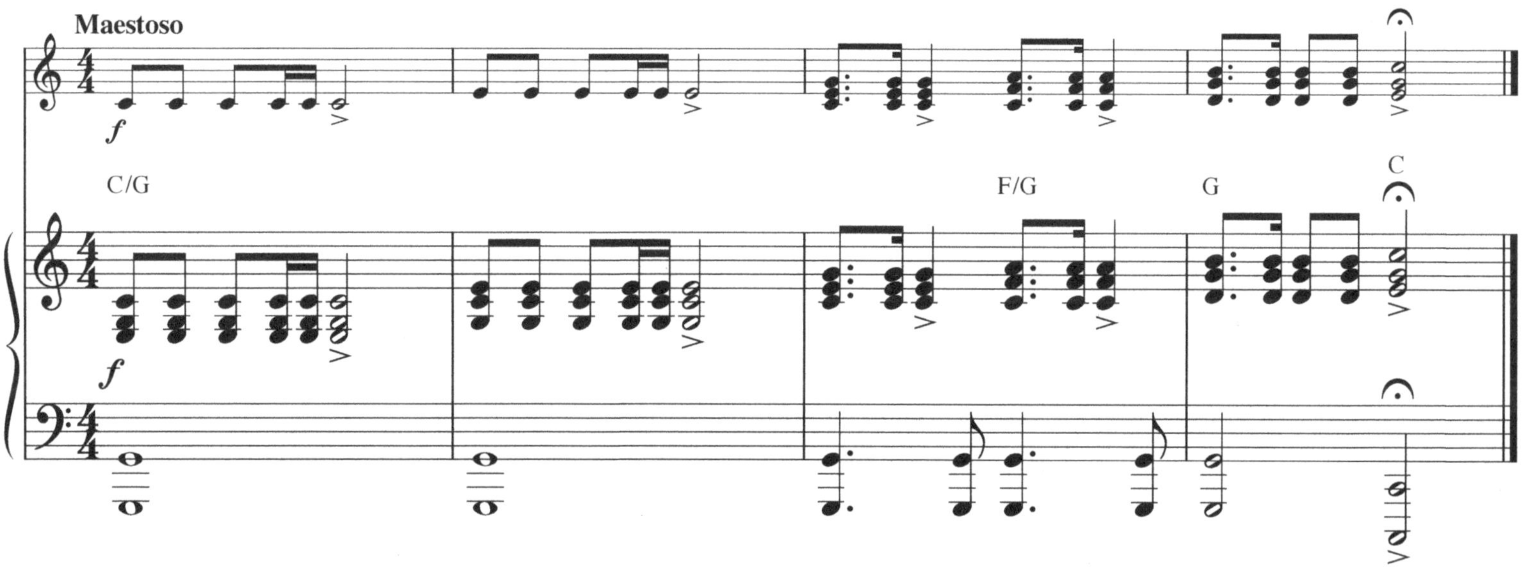


## 84. O TANNENBAUM

German Carol

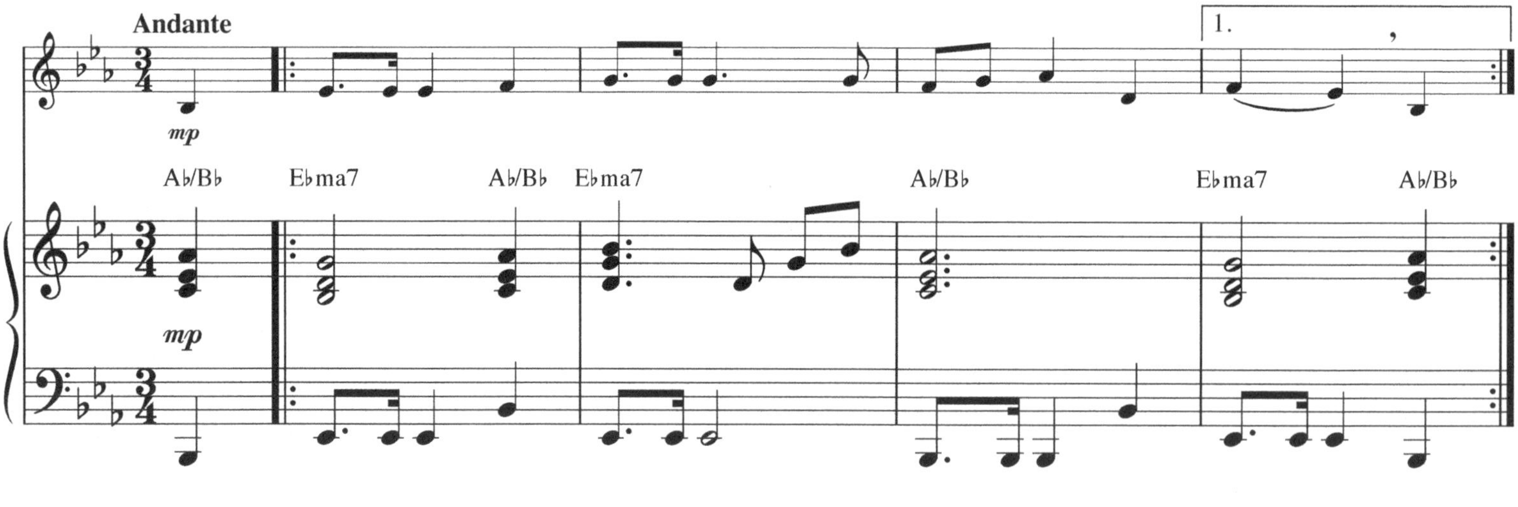

## 85. S'VIVON

Traditional Hanukkah Song

English Carol

## 86. GOOD KING WENCESLAS

*Student books have repeats, not 1st and 2nd endings.*

## 87. TONE BUILDER

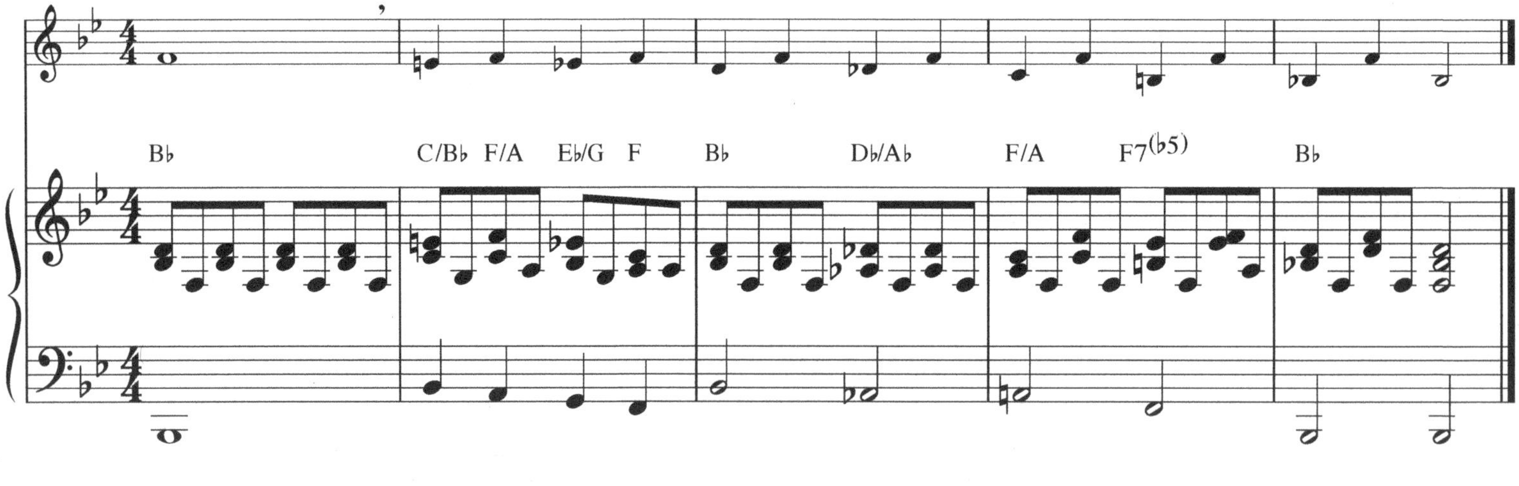

## 88. FLEXIBILITY STUDY

## 89. TECHNIQUE TRAX

## 90. CHORALE

Johann Sebastian Bach

## 91. TOREADOR SONG (from CARMEN)

Georges Bizet

## 92. LA CUMPARSITA

G. Rodriguez

## 93. THE YELLOW ROSE OF TEXAS

American Folk Song

## 94. SCALE STUDY

## 95. ADVANCE AUSTRALIA FAIR

Peter Dodds McCormick

## 96. ESSENTIAL CREATIVITY

## 97. AMERICAN PATROL

F. W. Meacham

## 98. ARIA (from MARRIAGE OF FIGARO)

Wolfgang Amadeus Mozart

## 99. THE STARS AND STRIPES FOREVER

John Philip Sousa

E♭
A♭
B♭7
17
E♭
G
Cmi
A♭mi/C♭
C♭
E♭
B♭7
E♭

## 100. SIGHTREADING CHALLENGE

## 101. RHYTHM RAP

*Student books have repeats, not 1st and 2nd endings.*

## 102. LAZY DAY

*Student books have repeats, not 1st and 2nd endings.*

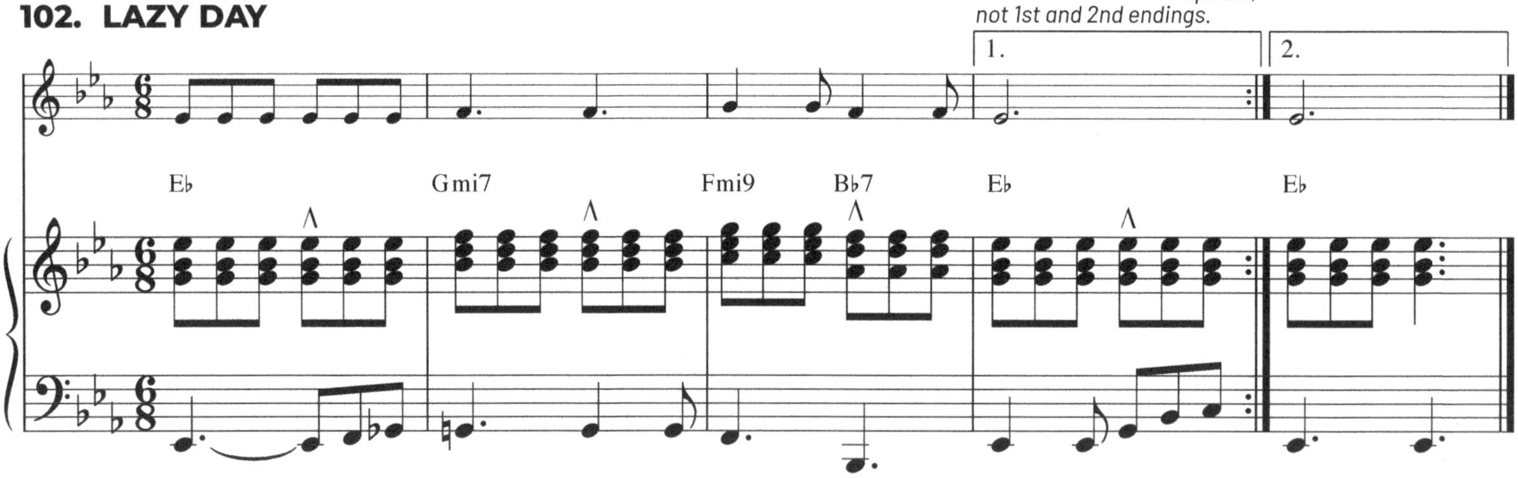

## 103. ROW YOUR BOAT

## 104. JOLLY GOOD FELLOW

## 105. CHANSON

French Folk Song

## 106. ESSENTIAL ELEMENTS QUIZ – WHEN JOHNNY COMES MARCHING HOME

American Folk Song

## 107. CHROMATIC SCALE

## 108. TECHNIQUE TRAX

## 109. HABAÑERA (from CARMEN)

Georges Bizet

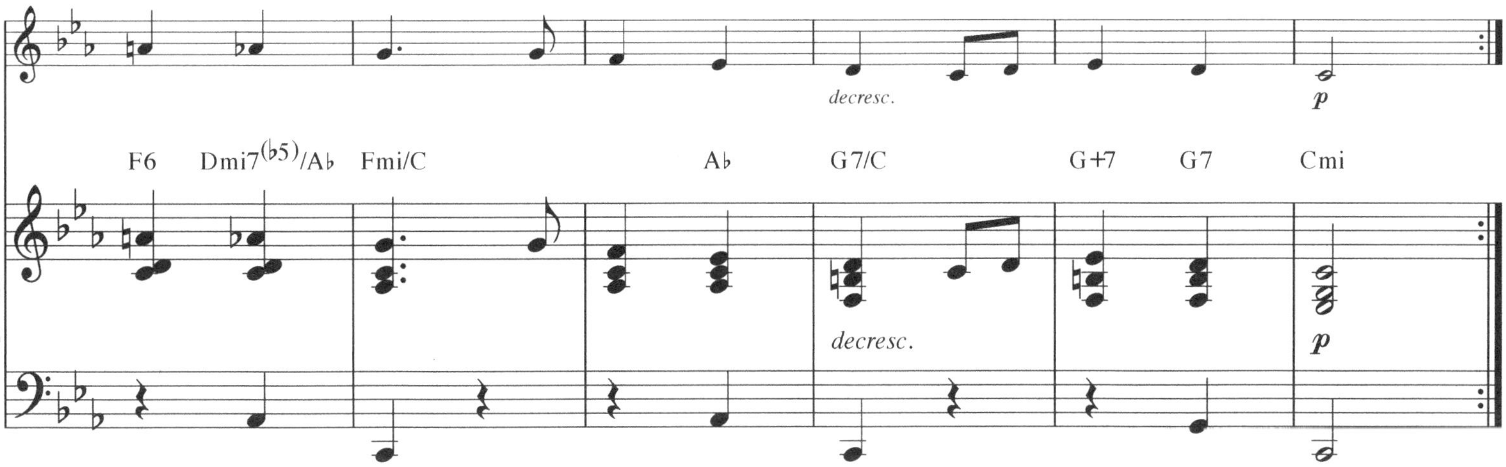


## 110. CHROMATIC CRESCENDO

## 111. TURKISH MARCH (from THE RUINS OF ATHENS)

Ludwig van Beethoven

## 112. THE OVERLANDER

Australian Folk Song

## 113. STACCATO STUDY

## 114. YANKEE DOODLE DANDY

George M. Cohan

## 115. SIGHTREADING CHALLENGE

## 116. RHYTHM RAP

## 117. THREE TO GET READY

## 118. TRIPLET STUDY

## 119. MARCH (from THE NUTCRACKER) – Duet

Peter I. Tchaikovsky

## 120. ESSENTIAL ELEMENTS QUIZ – THEME FROM FAUST

Charles Gounod

## 121. SCALE STUDY

## 122. OVER THE RIVER AND THROUGH THE WOODS

American Folk Song

## 123. RHYTHM RAP

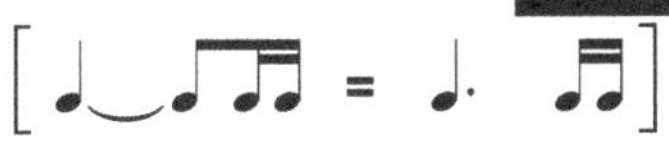

## 124. ON THE MOVE

## 125. HIGHER GROUND

## 126. ESSENTIAL ELEMENTS QUIZ

## 127. THE MARINES' HYMN

March Tempo

## 128. D.S. MARCH

March Tempo
N.C.
Bb7 Eb Ab Ao
Bb7 Eb F7 Bb7 Eb
Ab F7/A Eb/Bb Ab Bb7 Eb Cmi
Fine
D.S. al Fine
G7 Cmi G7 Cmi G7 Cmi Bb/F F7 Bb F7 Bb F7 Bb

## 129. CAN–CAN

Jacques Offenbach

## 130. TARANTELLA

Italian Folk Song

## 131. EMPEROR WALTZ

Johann Strauss, Jr.

## 132. ENGLISH DANCE – Duet

Johann Christian Bach

## 133. ESSENTIAL ELEMENTS QUIZ – BRITISH GRENADIERS

Traditional

## 134. NASSAU BOUND

Bahamian Folk Song

## 135. UNFINISHED SYMPHONY THEME

Franz Schubert

## 136. RHYTHM STUDY

## 137. COUNTRY GARDENS

English Folk Song

Allegretto

## 138. JOSHUA

African-American Spiritual

Allegro

## 139. LISTEN TO THE MOCKINGBIRD

Alice Hawthorne

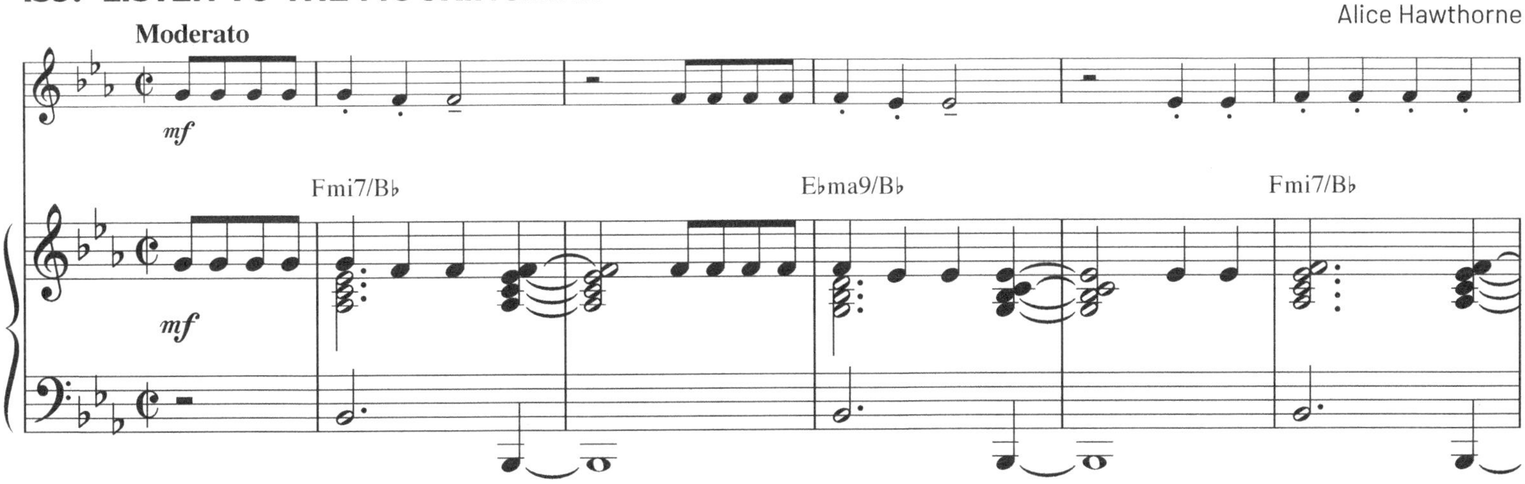


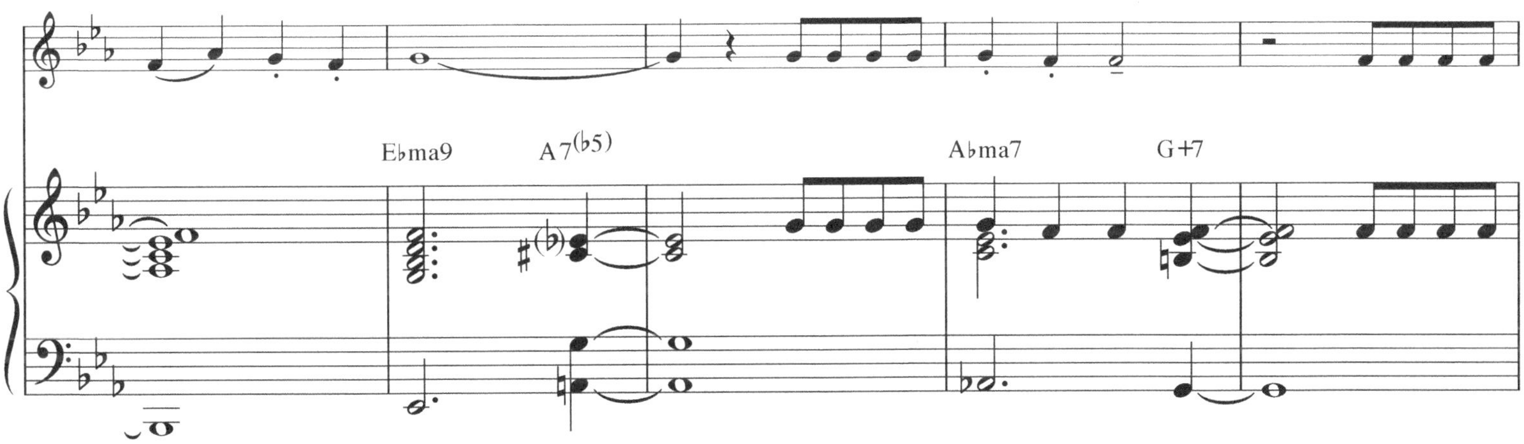


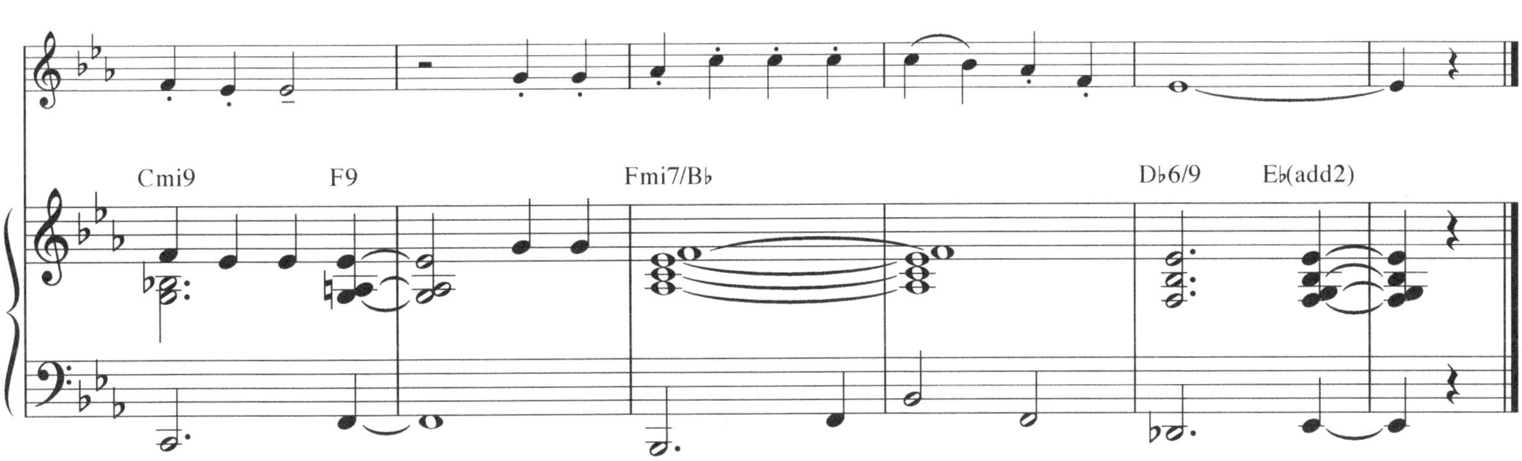

## 140. ANCHORS AWEIGH

Capt. A.H. Miles and C.A. Zimmerman

## 141. GREENSLEEVES

English Folk Song

## 142. THE LONG CLIMB

## 143. THE BLUE BELLS OF SCOTLAND

Scottish Folk Song

## 144. NATURAL MINOR SCALE

## 145. FINALE FROM "NEW WORLD SYMPHONY"

Antonin Dvorák

Student Book Page 30

## 146. HARMONIC MINOR SCALE

## 147. HUNGARIAN DANCE NO. 5

Johannes Brahms

## 148. POMP AND CIRCUMSTANCE (LAND OF HOPE AND GLORY)

Edward Elgar

## 149. SIMPLE GIFTS – Band Arrangement

Shaker Folk Song
Arr. by John Higgins

D.S. al Coda
mf
F/B♭
C 5/B♭
E♭ma9
F 5
Coda
20
Maestoso
rall.
ff
D♭/E♭
E♭
A♭
A♭/G
Fmi7
A♭/E♭
E♭5/D♭
Cmi7
A♭/C
E♭5/D♭
E♭5
rall.
A♭
D♭ma7
A♭
D♭ma7
B♭mi
Cmi7
B♭mi/D♭
E♭
D♭
B♭mi7
A♭
rall.

## 150. SEMPER FIDELIS – Band Arrangement

John Philip Sousa
Arr. by John Higgins

1.
2.
ff
B♭7
E♭
30
ff
sim.
B♭7
E♭
B♭7
38
E♭
B♭7
E♭
B7
E♭/B♭
B♭
E♭

Irish Folk Song
Arr. by John Higgins

## 151. DANNY BOY – Band Arrangement

18
mf a tempo
Bb Eb/F Bb Bb/D F/Eb Eb Ebma9 Eb Bb Bb/D Cmi7 Eb/F F Gmi Gmi/F
mf a tempo
26
mf
ff
Eb Bb/D Cmi F Bb Eb Cmi7
ff
30 Adagio
rit.
mp
p
rall.
Bells
Bb/D Gmi C7 N.C. Eb Bb
rit.
mp
p
rall.

## 152. TAKE ME OUT TO THE BALL GAME – Band Arrangement

By Jack Norworth and Harry von Tilzer
Arr. by John Higgins

21
mf
mf
Eb
Fmi7
Bb7
Eb7
Eb9
29
ff
Eb7
Db/F
Eb7/G
Ab
C7/G
Fmi
Ab
Ao
Eb/Bb
C7
ff
1.
2.
F7
Bb7
Eb
Bb7
Eb

## 153. SERENGETI (AFRICAN RHAPSODY) – Band Arrangement

John Higgins

27
mp
Gmi/B♭
E♭
mp
sim.
F
E♭/G
sim.
F
F/C
E♭
E♭/G
E♭/B♭
F/A
F
37
f
decresc.
mp rit.
G5
Csus2
Cma7/F
f
decresc.
mp rit.

45
Moderately Fast
Guiro
Scrape
f
Maracas or Shaker
Fmi6/A♭
Add Bongos or Tom-Tom
Triangle or Cowbell
49
Play 3 times
"Celebration"
Trumpet only 1st time
Add lower Brass 3rd time
Add W.W. 2nd time
E♭
f
Play left hand 3rd time only
Add Horn 1st time

57
mf decresc.
mf decresc.
65 Slowly "Sunset"
mp rit.
mp
Eb/Ab
Db6(b5)
Eb/Bb F5/Bb
mp rit.
mp
Eb/Bb
F5/Bb
Eb5 Db Fmi
Eb
F5 Eb
p
p

## 154. CHORALE (Concert B♭)

## 155. CHORALE (Concert E♭)

## 156. CHORALE (Concert F)

## 157. CHORALE (Concert Ab)

## 158. CHORALE (Concert C)

## KEY OF CONCERT B♭ MAJOR

## 159.

**160.**

B♭ F7sus B♭ E♭ F E♭ F B♭
Gmi F E♭ B♭/D Cmi7 B♭/D Cmi7 F B♭

**161.**

B♭ F B♭ E♭ F B♭

**162.**

B♭ Cmi/B♭ Dmi/B♭ E♭/B♭ E♭/F Dmi Cmi F7 B♭

Student Book Page 35

## KEY OF CONCERT E♭ MAJOR

**163.**

**164.**

**165.**

**166.**

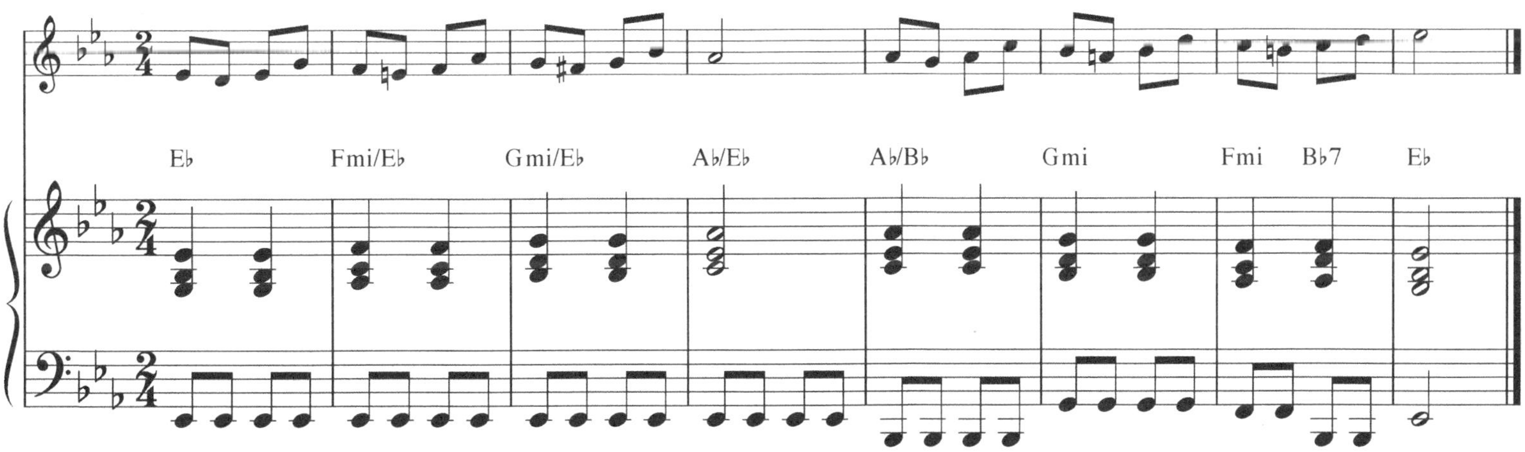


## KEY OF CONCERT F MAJOR

**167.**

**168.**

F
Gmi7/C
F
B♭
C
B♭(add2)
C
F

Dmi
C
B♭
F/A
Gmi7
F/A
Gmi7
C
F

**169.**

F
C7
F
B♭
C
F

**170.**

F
Gmi/F
Ami/F
B♭/F
B♭/C
Ami
Gmi
C7
F

## KEY OF CONCERT A♭ MAJOR

**171.**

**172.**

**173.**

**174.**

## KEY OF CONCERT C MAJOR

**175.**

**176.**

C
G7sus
C
F
G
F
G
C
Ami
G
F
C/E
Dmi7
C/E
Dmi7
G
C

**177.**

C
G7
C
F
G
C

**178.**

C
Dmi/C
Emi/C
F/C
F/G
Emi
Dmi
G7
C

## KEY OF CONCERT G MINOR

### 179.

### 180.

## KEY OF CONCERT C MINOR

**181.**

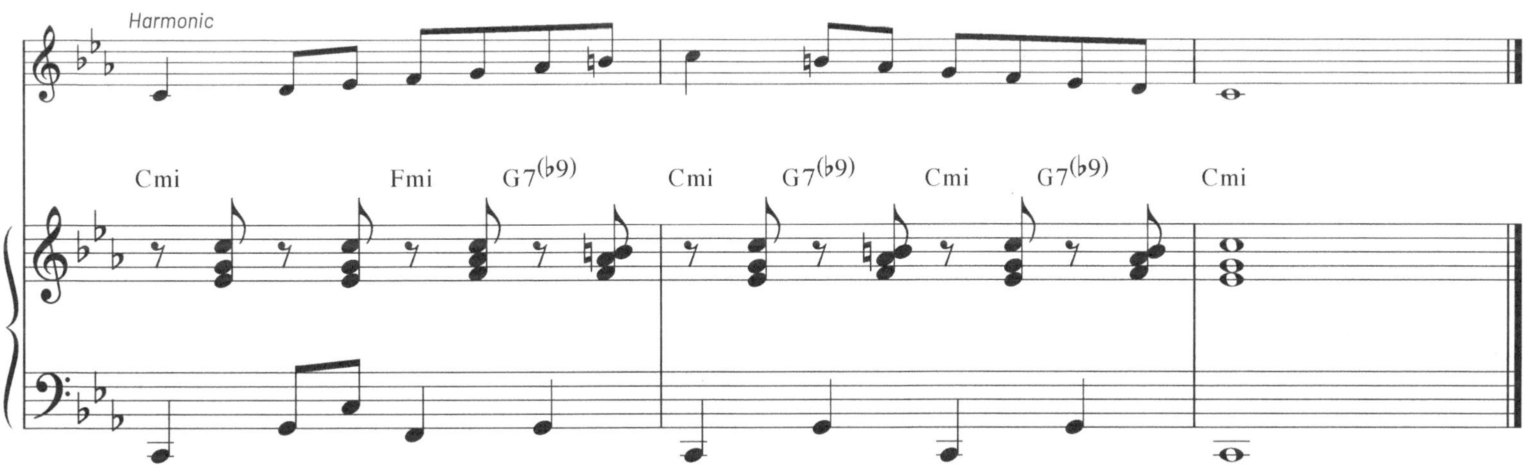


**182.**

## KEY OF CONCERT D MINOR

### 183.

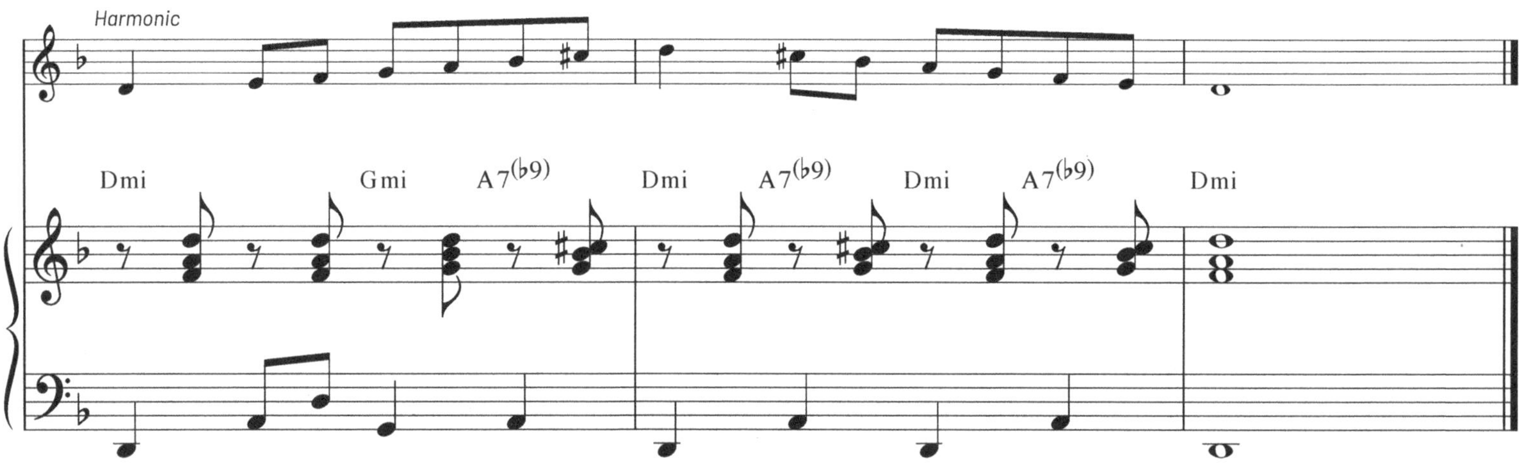


### 184.

## CHROMATIC SCALES

**185.**

**186.**

Haydn – Popp
Edited by H. Voxman

## RONDO – Finale – Flute Solo

f
f
27
Fine
sfz
sfz
sfz
sfz
sfz
sfz
f
f
D.S. al Fine (no repeat)

## ARIETTE from "Panurge" – Oboe Solo

A.E.M. Grétry
Arr. by H. Voxman

mp
p
f
47
p/pp
p/pp
sim.
1.
2.
56
f
mf
mf

## RONDO from "Suite in G" – Bassoon Solo

Paul Koepke

40
cresc. poco a poco
cresc. poco a poco
50

## HUNTERS' CHORUS from "Der Freischütz" – Clarinet Solo

Carl Maria von Weber
Arr. by Henry W. Davis

28
38

## MOSAIC – Alto Clarinet Solo

R. H. Walthew
Arr. by H. Voxman

31
p
p
f
sffz
p
f
p
p
f
1.
2.
p
f
p
f

## BOURRÉE from "First French Suite" – Bass Clarinet Solo

Johann Sebastian Bach
Arr. by R. Hervig

16
p
f
p
f
p
1.
2.
f
mf
rit.
f
(♮)

**SONATINA from "Divertimento #2" – Alto Saxophone Solo**

Wolfgang Amadeus Mozart
Arr. by H. Voxman

f
p
22
28
rit.

## PRESTO from "Trio V" – Tenor Saxophone Solo

Franz Josef Haydn
Arr. by H. Voxman

1.
2.
29
37
D.S. al Fine (no repeat)

## SARABANDE AND GAVOTTE – Baritone Saxophone Solo

Arrangelo Corelli
Arr. by H. Voxman

21
mf
cresc.
cresc.
f
f
1.
mf
2.
mf
30
mf
cresc.
cresc.
f
rit. (last time)
f rit. (last time)
1.
mf
2.

## VEGA – Trumpet Solo

Vander Cook

25
To Coda
Trio

45
p
mf
f
D. S. al Coda
Coda
accel.

## ROMANZE from "Concerto No. 3, KV 447" – F Horn Solo

Wolfgang Amadeus Mozart
Arr. by H. Voxman

opt.
22
26
30

34
opt.
p
37
mf
Ped.
Ped.
p
p
opt.
p rit.
pp
pp
rit.
ppp

## TURQUOISE – Trombone Solo

Vander Cook

13
Moderato (♩ = 96)
mp lightly
mf
mp
f
rit.
a tempo
mf a tempo

To Coda
33 Andante (♩ = 88)
D.S. al Coda
mp lightly
Coda
mf
f
accel.
ff

## GARNET – Baritone B.C./T.C. Solo

Vander Cook

Andante (♩ = 72)

25
p rit.
a tempo
p rit.
f a tempo
Moderato (♩ = 90)
p happily
p
f
p
f
p
p
rit.
f
a tempo
rit.
f
a tempo

To Coda
45
f
D.S. al Coda
p happily
Coda
p slower
mp
accel.
mf
mp accel.
f
faster

## IN THE HALL OF THE MOUNTAIN KING from "Peer Gynt Suite"

**Tuba/Electric Bass Solo**

Edvard Grieg
Arr. by G. E. Holmes

23
E. Bass 8va
f
mf
31

35 E. Bass loco
p
p
f
45 E. Bass 8va
p
pp
p
pp

## INTERMEZZO from "Carmen" – Orchestra Bells Solo

Georges Bizet
Arr. by Will Rapp

mp
3
mp
3
3
23
p
p
poco rit.
pp
poco rit.
pp
Ped.
Ped.

## GYPSY DANCE from "Carmen" – Xylophone Solo

Georges Bizet
Arr. by Will Rapp

21
ff
ff
mp
mp
ff
ff
mf
mf
31

41
50
f
f